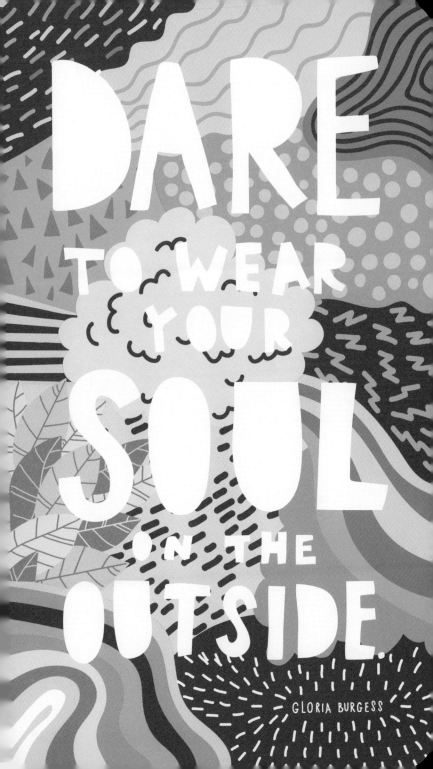

DARE TO WEAR YOUR SOUL ON THE OUTSIDE.

GLORIA BURGESS

CELEBRATE

your

CRAZINESS...

CELEBRATE

YOU.

Leo Buscaglia

BE OUTRAGEOUS.

GITA BELLIN

We're not meant to fit in. We're meant to STAND out.

SARAH BAN BREATHNACH

HERE'S TO THE
CRAZY ONES.
THE
MISFITS.
THE
REBELS.
THE
TROUBLEMAKERS.
THE
Round pegs
IN THE
SQUARE HOLES.

apple

BELIEVE in YOURSELF

and ALL that you ARE.

CHRISTIAN D. LARSON

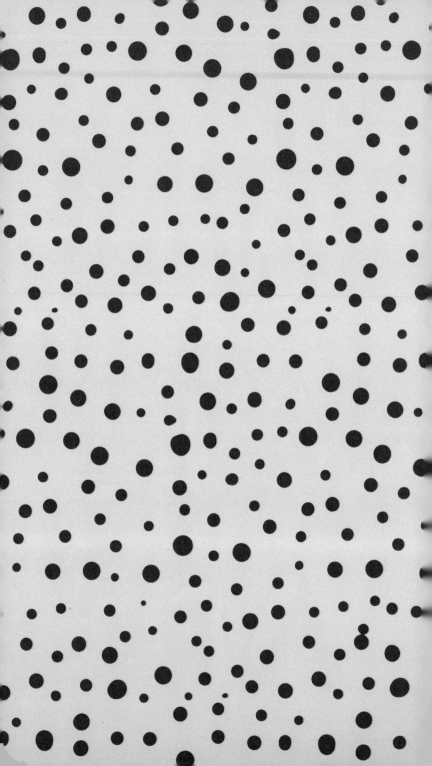

YOU ARE A
WONDERFUL
CREATION.

Oscar Wilde